Basic Life Manual

So You Don't Screw It Up

*"Practical Truths and Lifehacks
That Will Never Fail"*

S. Kent Garrett

WWW.TRUEVINEPUBLISHING.ORG

Basic Life Manual

S. Kent Garrett

Published by

True Vine Publishing Company

810 Dominican Dr.

Nashville TN 37228

www.TrueVinePublishing.org

ISBN: 978-1-968092-18-4 Paperback

ISBN: 978-1-968092-19-1 eBook

Printed in the United States of America.

For information, contact the author.

TABLE OF CONTENTS

INTRODUCTION

W hy read this book? It's got to be for reasons more than just to gain knowledge. Knowledge and insight are readily available in this digital age. There are multitudes of podcasts, commentaries, interviews, videos, and written works that offer superb insight into self-improvement— many just as good, if not better, than most things in this book. But this book will be different. Not because there's something inherently special in these pages, but because you will be different.

You're not going to just read to get another notch in the belt of wisdom. You will read every purposeful word with three things in mind: 1) What does this mean for me? 2) How can I use it? and 3) When will I use it?

The goal is to read this book slowly, without distractions. This is not a race to the finish line; the journey itself is the finish line. There will be no magical wisdom imparted to you once you finish reading. However, there will be magical wisdom imparted to you along the way—*if* you apply what you learn to your specific life situations.

Always remember: the objective is not just to get through the book, but to value and enjoy each step. Wisdom is defined as the application of truth to specific situations. So don't let your wisdom rot inside your mind. Use it. Master it. Teach it. *Be* it.

This book is like a top-of-the-line Swiss army knife. It's a wonderful tool—but useless if it's not put to work. Reading this book will give you the skills to use the tool, but it's still up to you to make the intentional decision to put in the effort. The writing style may also feel different or even suboptimal. I'll admit that I am not a seasoned professional when it comes to the intricacies of literary craft.

Still, I believe the content of this book is life-changing. So try to look past any oddities or less-than-ideal communication styles. What is "ideal" anyway? The ideal is just subjective conjecture, nonetheless.

Several topics in this book are drawn from my experiences as an end-of-life counselor. I've had dozens of intimate, cherished conversations with people in the final hours of their journey. I listened intently—for advice, regrets, wisdom, joy, stories, and final words. I've summarized and included what I've learned into practical applications throughout the book. My hope is that both you and I can benefit from the wisdom of our passing brothers and sisters.

I wrote this book for two reasons. First, I wrote it to remind myself of all the things I've learned over the last 20-plus years. Lessons that came from deep self-reflection and emotional exploration. Twenty years of studying psychology and philosophy in practical, everyday terms. Twenty years of making huge mistakes—hurting people, being selfish, giving in to addiction, destroying trust, being controlled by trauma, using people disrespectfully, choosing arrogance over love.

I've taken the insight given to me by people much smarter than myself and condensed it into a palatable set of principles. These are drawn from thousands of hours of counseling, mentorship, real-life successes and failures, broken relationships, impossibly hard conversations, moments of self-actualization, and examples from some of history's finest human accomplishments. These pages hold psychological and philosophical truths that can guide you toward becoming the best version of yourself. This isn't a motivational speech or coddling session to make you feel good. This is the scientific method of mental wellness—tested truths on how to win at life.

The second reason I wrote this book is to give you the secrets I had to learn the hard way—so you can use them *before* life forces you to. This is a simple journey meant to make your world a better place. A simple journey that can become complex if not given proper effort and intention. Some things may sound cliché or inspirational in a cheesy way. Still, I assure you, the principle behind them is time-tested and rock solid.

You'll see the evidence in the words of the greatest writers, philosophers, and historical figures referenced throughout each chapter. All of life is a set of choices. This is no different. What lies in front of you is a choice—a choice to read, learn, and act.

No matter who you are—whether you're earning eight figures a year or barely scraping by, whether you're living on cloud nine or battling crippling depression—this book is for you. It has everything you need to know *so you don't screw your life up.*

CHAPTER 1

FEAR REGRET MORE THAN FAILURE

Paralyzed. Not able to move. Thinking about what I desperately want but not being able to make my body move to get it. This is the perfect description of me on a dirty gym floor during a grade school dance.

I felt deep in my gut that I needed to go over and ask Cindy to dance. Nothing else in life mattered at that moment, just locking eyes and hands with her. Unfortunately, what I knew I needed to do wasn't what I wanted to do, because my desire to avoid embarrassment was greater than my desire to dance.

We've all been there, seeing a great opportunity right in front of our faces and then seeing the opportunity pass with only success happening in the imagination. The great Roman Stoic philosopher Seneca says that we suffer more in imagination than in reality. (Seneca. *Letters from a Stoic.*

Translated by Robin Campbell, Penguin Books, 1969, Letter 13). We also succeed more in imagination than in reality, but for different reasons. What I wish I had known on that dance floor in 8th grade and countless times afterward is that the pain and loss because of inaction far outweigh the potential failures of action. And trust me, many times in my life action has led to failure, embarrassment, lawsuits, loss of reputation or friendship, and turmoil in relationships. But those pale compared to the failure felt because of not even trying.

"It's better to love and have lost than never have loved at all." (Tennyson, Alfred Lord. *In Memoriam A.H.H.* 1850, section 27, line 15.) Awesome quote, but what the heck does that mean? Sounds like some nonsense cheap line in a second-rate Hallmark movie about unrealistic love in the big city. But the confusing quote is true, and it applies to all areas of life. The worst thing that could have hypothetically happened on that dance floor was a rejection and temporary humiliation. And even then, it would not have left me as defeated as I felt after knowing what I needed to do, but not even trying.

FEAR

Fear was in control, and when fear is in control, everything else takes a back seat. The key is understanding that in human beings, there will always be fear. Fear cannot and should not be eliminated. How we use fear to help meet our goals is a giant step towards self-growth and motivation. If you look at any great innovator or creator and peel back the onion layers, you will see that one driving motivator is the fear of being without. One can speculate that the invention of shoes was done out of fear of pain, the creation of modern medicine was done out of fear of death, and even the creation of the internet and social media was done, at least in part, because of the fear of missing out.

So how can we put a saddle on this unbroken beast that is fear and use it to help accomplish what we want? Fear is best viewed as an unexplored mile-wide pond. Uncertain of what lies beneath the surface, we rarely step into it. Take a courageous step, and you will find out that fear is a mile wide but only an inch deep.

Let's start with the loose definition of what fear is in the human context. Every human dies, and every species tries to prevent their own death. Our core motivations come from prolonging our lives and continuing the flourishing of our species. Fear is helpful in accomplishing this as it makes one aware of things that might impede our lives. These fears come as obvious things like avoiding immediate danger, removing ourselves from life-threatening situations, not harming ourselves or others, and so on. But fear also plays a role in more subconsciously, such as our need to be accepted by others, our avoidance of isolation, and the fear of being an outcast.

Luckily, today, in most modern societies, it is not a necessity to be part of a tribe to survive like it was in the past. But our primal brains still run on the need to be accepted.

So, what does this have to do with our programmed human fear of failure? Our brains think that if we fail, then we will be looked at as lesser and then not accepted by others and then we will have to fend for ourselves to find food, water, and shelter. And this simply is not a reality. Failure may mean temporary embarrassment or internal feelings of not being good enough, but failure will also drive motivation to try harder.

This is why most professional athletes will become better after a loss more than they will become better after a win. Failure isn't failure; failure is an opportunity to grow. Failure shouldn't be feared. In an ideal world it would be appreciated as the first step on a journey up the beautiful mountain that is success.

An example from two of the greatest basketball players of all time. Michael Jordan once told Shaq, according to an interview with Shaquille O'Neal himself, that before you succeed, you must first learn to fail. Wise words from one of the greatest athletes, so let's dive in and unpack what he means.

In sports psychology, it is common for an athlete to have a drop in performance if the athlete's goal is primarily centered on avoiding losing. To have the motivation to avoid a loss or failure usually results in failure itself. On the contrary, when someone is in the zone, as it is called, the possibility of failure is still real, but it is not in the athlete's mind. Instead, the athlete is focused on other things, such as the joy and passion of the game, visualizing success, or giving everything they have as competitive passion.

What was driving my thoughts on that dirty gym floor in 8th grade was all the ways I could fail. My passion for romance, giving Cindy a wonderful night, and my desire for connection all took a back seat to the fear of failure. His Airness Michael Jordan would say I didn't know how to fail, so I feared failure, and I feared the magnitude of the results of failure, which were only in my imagination and would never actually manifest in reality.

Dwayne "The Rock" Johnson was 15, and his family didn't have enough money for a Thanksgiving meal. While blessed with good genetics, he still struggled mightily financially and professionally. He is quoted as saying that when he was 23, he had two things: only $7 in his pocket and a desire to achieve. Injuries ended his college football career, and a Canadian professional football team eventually cut him. The story ends with his dedication and all his past failures, leading him to become one of the most famous and successful wrestlers and actors in the world.

So how did he get there? This story highlights the importance of using the multitude of past failures not to define a person but to propel a person into a future in which failure is still certainly a possibility, but it is not a fear.

So, fear of failure is a real thing, but it is self-limiting and needs to be understood. Once anxiety or fear has a name, then it loses its power. When we understand that fear of failure is designed to keep us safe but, in reality, it is self-defeating, then we can move forward in any action, be it professional or personal, in a way that reframes the whole idea of failure.

Training to fail is a common practice of weightlifters and Olympic athletes. If a muscle is forced to endure a stress that is greater than it can bear, then the muscle will adapt and grow. Psychological and social failure works the same way. The more we fail socially, the more we can learn; the more we learn, the better we become.

We must reframe failure from the common understanding it is innately bad to a new enlightened understanding that it can be very good. Most of the time, fear is False Evidence Appearing Real.

MOTIVATION

We now know that fear is motivating, should be motivating, and will always motivate. With that in mind, let's turn our attention to the fear of regret. And in this context the fear of regret will be positioned towards motivation to act.

We all have regrets, whether it's a DUI or treating someone poorly or choosing the wrong job. However, all these past mistakes have led you to exactly where you are at this very moment. Reading this book with whatever hairstyle you have and in whatever setting you are in.

So, all the "mistakes" or "regrets" are actually stepping stones to a learning experience that made you who you are today in this very moment. Few people intentionally try to screw their life up. We are all just doing the best we can with the amount of knowledge and understanding we have. Every experience in the past, be it good or bad, has made us who we are.

With that view of failure in mind let's look at how to apply this wisdom practically. Failure is growth in most contexts. But one of the hardest things to grow from is the act of not doing anything.

So, let the fear of missing out motivate you more than the fear of messing up. But what does missing out actually look like? There's wisdom in missing out on some things, such as a bad investment, an activity that will cause financial or personal stress on you or your family, hurting someone or something, and many more things.

I'm not advocating that you do everything and eventually get burnt out and hooked on some substance. If you're reading this book, then you probably have an idea of what you need to be doing and what you need to be avoiding.

Actually, you have more than just an idea; you have a deep gut conviction of what gives you purpose and meaning and what is also just frivolous pleasure that results in little progress. What I'm saying is that when you feel that gut conviction to be the person that you truly are, be it.

But why do you be that person? You be it because you know that's who you are, and you know that fearing failure is your body trying to protect you from something that doesn't exist.

You know that missing out on this action will cause more pain and suffering than acting and failing ever would. So next time you're in a situation where you need to have a difficult conversation, courageously meet someone, tough out a difficult work dilemma or find a new job, stand up for something you believe in, set goals to improve mental health, or whatever situation that requires your action, think about what you will feel like after the situation is over if you don't act.

And let that motivate you to do whatever is needed. Failure is temporary; growth lasts forever.

Let's finish this chapter with the all-important case study we started with. If eighth-grade me understood what I know now, then my fear of regret would have greatly outweighed my fear of failure.

I would have looked across the gym floor and locked eyes with Cindy. I would have thought of what I would feel like tomorrow morning if I had not asked her to dance. I would have let that deep sadness of regret motivate me to walk across that floor and ask her to dance.

I would have known that even if she said no, I would have grown and gained courage just for asking. I would have known that there really is no reason to fear failure and that wisdom is how not to screw your life up.

CHAPTER 2

BE WHERE YOUR FEET ARE

Lying on the couch watching TV, beautiful brunette hair stretches across my chest, a beating heart just inches away from mine. True connection was possible, yet it was just out of grasp. My mind wanted to be elsewhere, wanted to be scrolling endlessly through social media to see what little spike of dopamine my brain could get over and over. Wanted to escape to a greener field just out of sight.

Pure euphoric bliss was knocking down my door, and all I wanted to do was run out of the house. I can count on two fingers the number of girls I've truly, romantically, selflessly loved. The beautiful brunette hair stretched across my chest belonged to one of them. Hindsight is 20/20, but I'll be damned if, in this case, it isn't 20/10.

What could cause someone to want something they don't have when everything they've ever wanted is right beside them? The answer is simple yet very difficult to understand. When I was a child, I was praised for my achievements; an A in a class was rewarded with an expectation to get an A in the next class.

A home run in baseball was celebrated by visualizing what I will do in my next at bat. So, naturally, any sense of accomplishment or achievement was short-lived and followed by the necessity of achieving something new and different.

Developmental psychologist Dr. Benjamin Houltberg calls this "performance-based identity" (Houltberg, Benjamin J. "Self-Narrative Profiles of Elite Athletes and Comparisons on Psychological Well-Being." *Journal of Applied Sport Psychology*, vol. 31, no. 4, 2019, pp. 469-485.).

This achievement-based identity plagued my adult life as well. Nothing was good unless it was novel, nothing was achieved unless there was something else also to be achieved. Having a sense of happiness and joy was met with the internal feeling of needing to go somewhere where the grass was even greener while ignoring the grass I was standing on. This, as I found out, is a sick, twisted delusion that ultimately leads to pain and suffering.

When you reach the greener grass on the other side of the field, you look up and see greener grass in front of you. You feel you must find it. When you get to this greener grass, you look up and see greener grass off in the distance.

PARADOX OF CHOICE

One would assume that many choices would lead to making the best choice and being content with that decision. However, the opposite is usually the outcome. Enter the paradox of choice.

Psychologist Barry Schwartz describes having an excess of choices as leading to an increase in anxiety. With more options, individuals fear making the wrong choice, leading to post-decision regret. They might continually second-guess their decisions, wondering if another option would have been better (Schwartz, Barry. *The Paradox of Choice: Why More Is Less.* Harper Perennial, 2004, p. 89-108).

More choices lead to more dissatisfaction. Schwartz provides a solution. He states that the person choosing also has the power to be content with good enough or to strive to make the best choice. He found those who choose the good enough option are usually more content with their decision, possibly because a best possible choice is rarely realistic.

According to Schwartz, this is how you should make choices: seek satisfaction, not maximization; limit options; set realistic expectations; practice gratitude; and simplify decisions.

ACHIEVEMENT-BASED IDENTITY

Modern culture is plagued with achievement-based identity. When asked how much money is enough, John D. Rockefeller answered, "Just a little bit more." This attitude is widespread in Western culture and even praised in society, but eventually will lead to a constant feeling of lack and a desperate need for more. And more will never be enough.

So how do we escape this black hole of suckage that is achievement-based identity? Being present is the first step.

What if your life right in this very moment is as good as it ever will be? Really, actually this moment right now is the best your life will ever be. Are you ok with that, or does that give you a pit of sickness in your stomach?

Wanting something more in imagination than what you have in front of you right now is like lying on a beach and wanting to be in the mountains, and then going to the mountains and wanting to be back on the beach. Contentment will never come if we wish away the present moment.

Now, it is great to have goals, and it's great to meet those goals. But the odds are that for every goal you set, there will be some you will not achieve. So, basing your identity on meeting goals will inevitably lead to feeling like a failure.

The past is a memory, the future a possibility, and all that we have in reality is the present. It seems to be human nature to hope for the future and neglect the present.

When I was lying on that couch with everything I've ever wanted lying beside me, my mind felt like a hostage, desperately looking for any avenue of escape. Anxiously avoiding appreciating the present moment, clinging to some possibility of novelty that would soothe my present illusion of despair.

CHERISHING APPRECIATION

Why is it we only appreciate something after it's gone? Why is it so hard to love and cherish what we have with us right now?

Why is it that we curse the sun after a day spent in it but pray for sunlight after a week in the rain? Right here, right now, we need to make a covenant promise. I promise not to overlook the things I have hoping to gain something more.

The food in the fridge, the roof overhead, the shoes on my feet, the air in my lungs, and the love of another human being are all nothing short of miracles.

The key to happiness is to appreciate and truly love what you have right now and to consider anything you might gain simply a bonus. We suffer more in imagination than in reality, we succeed more in imagination than reality, and we are desperate more in imagination, which leads to being desperate in reality.

Presence brings contentment, and contentment brings the feeling of lack to an end. And, on a side note, it's nearly impossible to be content with the present moment while nose-deep in a phone screen. Put it down.

Present mindfulness is noticing the beauty around you right now: the laugh of a child, the cool of the breeze, the taste of food, the majesty of the sunset, the emotion in the voice of a loved one, the breath in your lungs.

Too often, we neglect the magnificent splendor all around us because our heads are down or our minds are in the future.

Three things that destroy contentment are noise, hurry, and busyness. Be mindful of these presence-breakers.

Modern technology is designed to limit your attention span, thus taking away your strength. Don't let this happen; fight against instant gratification and pleasure-seeking from screen time.

Now, let's talk about what reality is and what imagination is. What are good desires, and what is frivolous chasing after the wind?

The desires for self-improvement, growth, financial stability, improving the quality of life for yourself and those around you, providing a meaningful service to society, and freely expressing your passions are all good desires. But these are poor identities.

It is a great and noble act to try to make the world a better place, but there will be times—sometimes long periods—when you do not make the world a better place.

And if this is your sole identity, then you will succumb to the feeling of being a failure.

So, what is a good identity? The breath in your lungs, the beating of your heart, the thoughts in your mind at this very moment, being made in the image of God or whatever you choose to believe.

That cannot be taken from you, and that will never fail. You have no choice but to be content if all you want is what you already have.

REALITY VERSUS IMAGINATION

Everything that's ever happened to you in the past cannot be changed. It's easy to say that everything in the past is a learning experience, but let's look at what it actually, mentally, is.

Your past is a set of beliefs. Let's take, for example, an illustrated case study.

Two people are riding in the back of a car on the way to work. Out of nowhere, a pickup truck T-bones the car, sending it rolling down the street and tumbling into a roadside ditch.

Both people in the car survived. Stricken with terror, anxiety, and flashbacks, one person develops a coping mechanism of drinking and narcotics to relieve the pain.

The other person uses the injuries he suffered as motivation to get into shape to protect his body better and talk to others about the importance of safety belts and always being aware while driving.

He wants to learn more about why he is struggling with PTSD and enrolls in psychology courses. This leads him to develop a psychological defense system strategy and give talks on empowerment after traumatic events.

Two people are in the same situation; one is battling addiction while the other is giving TED Talks on his empowering experience. The past is an idea, and ideas can be molded.

The future is an idea—countless ideas. Most of which will never happen.

So, you can see that putting most of our energy into the past or the future is a complete garbage bin of waste.

What I wish I knew lying on that couch with the love of my life right next to me was that at that specific time, my life would never get any better than it was in that moment— and that I should be more than OK with that.

So the next time you feel anxious, worried, or that you're not doing enough, stop, take a breath, look at your feet, get rid of any thoughts of what you should be doing, and focus on the next thing you can actually do.

CHAPTER 3

WHAT IS YOUR "WHY"?

"The person who has a 'why' to live for can bear almost any 'how.'" (Frankl, Viktor E. *Man's Search for Meaning*. Beacon Press, 2006.)

Viktor Frankl was a psychologist and prisoner of war during World War II in Nazi Germany. During his imprisonment, he wrote in stunning detail about the great horror he suffered and the eventual reframing of hope by the camp prisoners. As one can imagine, living conditions in these camps were sadistically inhumane. Even the basic human right—the right to life—was not given. These prisoners didn't know if they or their families would be alive at the end of the day or even the end of the hour.

So, what was their purpose, what was their hope, what gave their life meaning? Frankl gives many examples of finding peace in the mundane. In one such example, he described holding a small piece of bread in the pocket of his prison uniform. For him, this little morsel of food acted as a source of contentment because it was his, and no one could take that from him.

His job, clothes, home, family, and respect had been taken from him, but that small clump of bread belonged to him and was a possession that he had full control of. He also points out that the prisoners' deaths were predictable based on their level of hopelessness. He says that various sicknesses caused death, but hopelessness caused the sickness. A prisoner's perception of having nothing to live for was almost always a terminal diagnosis.

Frankl's experience taught him a great deal about joy. He states that joy was found when a person found meaning in the task that he was given and not in circumstances outside of their control. Much like concerning oneself with circumstances and details outside of one's control leads to feelings of hopelessness and, ultimately, depression and anxiety.

He illustrated that when the men found purpose and meaning in the job they were doing and realized that the man beside them depended on them to do that job effectively, then there was a sense of joy and motivation even in these cruelest of human conditions. If joy and contentment are possible in a concentration camp, then it is possible for you wherever you are right now.

THREE ROADS TO PURPOSE

But why? Why did those prisoners choose purpose? How did they find it?

The first reason is that they chose to care not about themselves but about the people around them who depended on them. Whether their job was digging trenches, nailing railroad spikes in the freezing cold while being frostbitten, serving food, or simply communicating with others—if they focused on how their actions were affecting other people, then a sense of purpose naturally appeared.

Gandhi said, "The best way to find yourself is to lose yourself in the service of others." (Gandhi, Mahatma. *The Collected Works of Mahatma Gandhi*. Publications Division Government of India, 1958, vol. 45, p. 62.)

This doubles down when trying to find joy and meaning in addition to purpose. To put one's focus outside of oneself inherently brings a sense of motivation and obligation for good.

The first why to understand in your own life is: why do you influence or impact those around you? Why do you care how your life impacts others? Because in some form, someone depends on your actions and needs you to be the person you know you are supposed to be.

Whether it's as complicated as caring for a spouse or as simple as the fast-food worker needing a smile from you, there is always someone who needs you. And if you feel like no one needs you, first realize that is a lie, and second, take a walk downtown in the nearest city and see how many people could be positively affected by your simplest actions.

The second reason those prisoners chose contentment and purpose is that when they had everything taken away from them, they understood that one's mental energy is wasted worrying about things outside of one's control.

The Stoic philosophers had the phrase *"ta eph'hemin, ta ouk eph'hemin"*—what is up to us, what is not up to us. Discerning what is inside and outside one's control takes intentional effort, but it's not all that difficult to understand.

I can't decide who will win the next presidential election, but I can decide what clothes I will wear tomorrow. I can't control what happens to me necessarily, but I can control how I will respond to it.

Concentration camp prisoners couldn't control when they would be—or if they would be—released, how they were treated, or even if they would live or die, but they could control their mental attitude in response to the inhumane treatment. And they figured out no one could rid them of that piece of human dignity.

To a much lesser extent, we may not be able to control how a boss treats us, the sad ending to a relationship, how someone feels, or the actions a person takes. But we sure as hell can control what we do about it.

No one can ever offend us without our permission, and nothing can take away our ability to choose our thoughts and actions.

Listen, some things in this life are unfair. They don't make sense and just plain suck. True strength is found in understanding you can't change this.

You must accept this as reality and move forward with integrity—unwavering integrity of who you are and what you stand for. Even, for example, if your boss treats you poorly, you control how you respond to this, and in effect, your perception dictates this reality.

Some may see a rude, demeaning, arrogant jerk—but you see a learning tool you can use to become a better boss in your own life. Trials are not our masters; they are our tools.

The third reason these prisoners had motivation and purpose is because they faced a reality that life is temporary. They faced, almost daily, human death. While this may seem morbid and hopeless, it is actually freeing and empowering.

Let me explain. They understood better than most that their lives could end at any moment. With this understanding came a deep appreciation for every living moment and gratitude for the mundane, ordinary things life offers.

On the surface, it would seem that when faced with the reality of death, the fear of death would increase. But paradoxically, when something is brought to a certain reality and understands the fear—in this case, death—that fear then stops having power.

One prisoner whose feet were so frostbitten that he couldn't feel them found joy in finding something that resembled a string so he could close his shoes a little bit to escape from the pain. With the realization of life's fleeting, temporary nature, so comes the understanding that nothing is truly deserving of fear outside of the maker of the universe itself.

TWO-DAY TERMINAL DIAGNOSIS

An example from time itself to illustrate this third point. Imagine getting a 100% correct terminal diagnosis that you had less than two days to live. No cure and no extension possible.

Put the book down right now and think of the first few things you would do after hearing this news… What would happen to your mind?

Many fears—such as the fear of public speaking, public approval, shyness, worry about finances, and feeling the need to argue or debate—all would fly out the window. Life's meaning and purpose would become substantially greater because every moment would be calculated, and every second would have a deep meaning.

Every one of us has this diagnosis, but the perception is misunderstood. In a universe that is billions of years old, 80, 90, or even 100 years is just a blink in the eyes of eternity. So, all of our lives are just a blink.

The only difference between having a two-day terminal cancer diagnosis and being in good health in your 20s, 30s, or 40s is perception—not reality. We all have a two-day terminal diagnosis; we just don't live like it.

So, what is your why? Why do you do the things that you do? A life devoid of understanding why things are important will be a life without meaning.

What I wish I knew before I screwed my life up is why and how other people are depending on me. Why should I only devote thought space to things in my control? And with my "two-day terminal diagnosis," why should I make the most of every moment?

Tim McGraw was onto something when he sang, "Live like you were dying."

CHAPTER 4

DESIRE BRINGS LACK

All I wanted for my 10th birthday was a Pokémon card. Specifically, a holographic 1st edition Charizard card. Some of you may know what I'm talking about, and others may not understand. But these cards were the top of the top during the years of my childhood.

I remember inviting my classmates to my birthday party at a skating rink and biding the time until it was time to open presents. I hardly remember hanging out with my friends that day or even enjoying the skate park. But I remember opening that small gift bag and seeing that glowing lizard printed on the front of a trading card in a plastic protective case.

In my college years, I put an extraordinary amount of time and effort into finding a relationship and making sure that relationship didn't end. My motivation and desire were to have someone who was there for me and who I could depend on—or, more accurately, be co-dependent with.

I grew up with the fear of abandonment and attachment issues from my childhood needs of acceptance, nurturing, and belonging not being met. But this chapter isn't about the complex dynamics of childhood psychology. It's about how desire can bring motivation and how it more commonly brings unhappiness.

The great German philosopher Arthur Schopenhauer wrote, "The longing for what we do not possess reveals an inherent dissatisfaction with our present situation, showing how desire can be both a motivator and a source of suffering." (*The World as Will and Representation*, trans. E. F. J. Payne, Dover Publications, 1966, vol. 1, p. 196.)

When a toddler sees another child playing with a toy, he immediately forgets what he may have in his hand or what is around him and is solely focused on getting the toy that the other child is enjoying. Jealousy is an emotion that does not have to be taught.

But even desires not brought out of jealousy can create a lack of contentment if not well understood and guided. Humans are complex creatures, yet we haven't figured out how to appreciate what is around us while simultaneously desiring something we don't have. We're all still toddlers wanting the toy another kid has.

When the mind feels a need for something it does not have, it primally makes this need a priority above all else. This primal concept is stated before and is great for a preindustrial human without food and requires the desire to hunt and kill for survival.

But this adaptive psychology is not so great for someone with their basic human needs met and wants to keep up with the Joneses or live like the people they see on social media. This inherently good desire then turns into a feeling of inadequacy and comparison.

"Desire is a manifestation of a void, a lack in our current state, driving us to seek fulfillment from external sources." (Lacan, Jacques. Écrits: *A Selection*, trans. Alan Sheridan, Norton, 1977, p. 286.)

Imagine a person who desired nothing—literally nothing outside of what keeps them alive. You would think this person would be apathetic and stoic with no joy or happiness. But a person who desires nothing outside of what they already have and can also appreciate the beauty of life and humanity would be a person free from anxiety and full of joy.

People like Mother Teresa, Gandhi, Buddha, the Dalai Lama, Socrates, and many others exemplify this principle. Desiring nothing and being at peace with everything may not be possible in this life because human emotions are real and ever-changing.

But to be a little more joyful and a little less anxious, try to identify things you don't have and that you want, and meditate on how important those things really will be in 30 or 50 years. The key is to desire what you have access to right now—desire what you have, not what you don't have.

WIND

Desire can be a good thing, as we saw in Chapter 2, dealing with desire and identity, but it is not at all a good thing if your efforts are spent constantly thinking about and working towards something you don't have.

Had I enjoyed the moment at that skate park and been happy spending time with friends and cherishing moments with family, then maybe I would have memories of that instead of only remembering getting the one thing I didn't have—a thing that has now been sold and ultimately was unimportant.

"When we desire something intensely, it often reflects a lack within us, a feeling that we are incomplete without the object of our desire." (Fromm, Erich. *The Art of Loving*. Harper Perennial, 2006, p. 98.)

Let's attack that lie right now. What makes a person complete?

Similar to identity, if you feel that things outside of who you are make you complete, then you will live an incomplete life of comparison and envy.

Sometimes, you get satisfaction and contentment from outside sources—fun events, life changes or work accomplishments, buying a house, accomplishments of friends or family members, or many other things. And all these things are beautiful, wonderful parts of life, but they are just wind.

And the wind will stop blowing eventually. Leaving you in desperate need to chase after the wind.

Everything outside of oneself is an uncontrollable, unpredictable chasing after the wind. So figure out who you are, what you stand for, and what makes you *you*, and go after that.

HAPPY

In 2009, I went on a weeklong trip to a rural area of Haiti about two hours outside of Port-Au-Prince towards Saint-Marc. Each day, we would ride in the back of a pickup truck for an hour over what would not qualify as a road in most of the developed world to the top of a hillside.

On this hillside was a community of inhabitants without running water, electricity, or even sufficient shelter. The kids ran around the grassy hillside with no clothes, and the parents had no form of transportation. They lived lifestyles with no luxury or amenities. These were some of the happiest people I have ever encountered.

I found out through living with them that there was only contentment left when they did not desire what they did not have. They were not aware of what other cultures were like, so comparison was not possible.

These people had unlocked the secret of happiness in their poverty. They couldn't compare or feel inadequate. They put their heart into what they had and caring for those around them. Their needs were met, and that was all they needed to be happy.

Think of something that you wanted at one point in your life. For some people, it's money; for others, fame, a nice house, car, clothes, success in business, an attractive spouse, or many other things. For me, it was fame and notoriety.

I thought that if I was famous and everybody knew me, then everyone would respect me, and I would have much fewer problems and feel happy. As we can see with many famous people, this is not true.

Studies show that famous people are usually more generally unhappy than the general population. This is in part due to constant stress and scrutiny. (Buchtel, Emma A., et al. "The Dark Side of Fame: Psychological and Societal Implications." *Journal of Happiness Studies*, vol. 21, no. 4, 2020, pp. 987–1005.)

But why does fame actually not bring happiness? Because happiness isn't a destination; it's a journey. This is foundational.

Happiness doesn't just appear when we achieve a goal or reach a destination. True happiness doesn't come, for example, when you close on the house or marry that special person. These are wonderful achievements, but they are just wind.

Happiness comes when you learn to find meaning in the rocky years before the marriage, or when you see the fruitful benefits of the financial struggles before buying the house that led you to think being a homeowner wasn't possible.

Happiness comes from a change in perception— to see the fights after the wedding day and the hardships of raising the kids as part of the beauty of life's journey. Happiness is found in appreciating everything life offers, such as appreciating a divorce as a learning and growing experience to make you stronger.

Happiness is waking up every day and being thankful for any challenge and even the pain and suffering you might face.

Happiness is found when you deal with depression and battle anxiety and reframe your mindset from being a victim suffering to being a warrior becoming stronger through the unfair adversity you are facing.

Life sucks, friend; life sucks for everyone. But life doesn't decide if we are happy—we do. We have complete control and power to decide how we respond to the sadness and struggle of life.

Pause. Read that last paragraph again.

All that is great in theory but hard to practice. So, what can you do today?

One thing to do today is to list or think about things you don't have that you desire. Then, understand why you want each thing listed. Will this thing be important in 50 years, or is it just something you want out of comparison or feelings of inadequacy?

Thus, understanding and naming each desire will let you have power over it.

The key to happiness is simple, but it's also a choice. A choice that you must make every day: will you choose happiness or continue to live how the world says you should live?

Will you appreciate the things that you do have, enjoy the beauty that the world and humanity offer, and understand each desire you have as potentially leading to the desperate feeling of lacking and needing something?

At this point in your life, you know that your identity and self-worth do not come from anything that you don't have or anything that is outside of who you are.

And that's what I wish I had known at my 10th birthday party before I messed it up.

CHAPTER 5

GO GET IT

I was a shy kid, a little insecure, and I never wanted to be a burden. I felt like any time I expressed my needs, I disappointed someone. If I didn't ruffle anyone's feathers or muddy the water at all, then I felt okay. It was okay if I was uncomfortable because I felt like I could handle it, but if I made someone else feel uneasy, then I felt like a failure.

This still plagues me occasionally in adulthood, too. Just last week, I bought a dozen eggs only to realize one was broken at the checkout counter. Instead of holding the rest of the customers up, I decided to ignore it and deal with a broken egg instead of going back to get a fresh dozen. We'll call it kindness and justify it by saying I was putting others' needs above my own. But it used to be much worse. It used to paralyze me.

One summer day during my preteen years, I went to an antique show festival with my dad, brothers, and grandparents. I remember only a little about the pageantry and setup of the event and what we did that day. I remember one specific booth giving away free pocketknives to anyone who would talk to the people at the booth.

I glanced sheepishly at the knife as I walked past but couldn't muster the courage to get one. I couldn't find the boldness or the confidence to get something that was free. At the end of the day, we walked back to the car, ready to head out. While I was talking to my brother about what cool things happened and what I liked, I said that I wished I could have gotten one of those knives.

Overhearing this, my grandfather looked at me and said a simple sentence he may not have thought twice about but one that has never left my mind: "If you want it, go get it."

Could it be that simple? What if they don't have any more, or if they won't give me one, or if they laugh in my face and say I'm too young to have one? What if they try to get into a conversation with me and make me nervous? Every good decision ever made resulted from someone moving past the what-ifs.

Up to this point, most of the content in the book has been centered on accepting what you can't control and focusing on what you can, along with the wisdom to know the difference. We've talked about why present mindfulness is important and how to use and perceive fear as positive and helpful. And now we will discuss how to act on things in your control.

Let's start with the difference, as Steven Covey says in *The Seven Habits of Highly Effective People*, between the circle of influence and the circle of control. Things that we can influence are factors and situations that are in our control and deserve action. Concerning situations are usually worth being aware of but are not influential and deserve attention but not action.

I may be concerned about influenza, but I cannot stop or eliminate it. I can, however, act in ways that will influence whether I or my direct family get or spread it. "Proactive people focus their efforts on the Circle of Influence. They work on the things they can do something about: health, children, problems at work. Reactive people focus their efforts on the Circle of Concern. They focus on the weaknesses of other people, the problems in the environment, and circumstances over which they have no control." (*Covey*, p. 82).

ACT ON THE RIGHT THINGS

Now it's time for a deep, introspective look inside yourself. It's fine to tell you to act on things you can influence, but how do you act? I can't prescribe that specifically for you because action looks different for every person.

If you wanted to build a bridge, you wouldn't tell a structural engineer and a brick mason to act in the exact same way. The same goes for life. So, you need to deeply understand what your core values and features are and never sway from them.

You must stand for what is valuable to you and what you hold dear to your heart. Some examples from my life are protecting the innocent and vulnerable, providing counsel for those in need or hurting, physical and mental well-being for myself and my family, gaining knowledge and wisdom to share it with others, providing resources to those in need, and many more things.

But my list cannot and should not be exactly like yours. The world would be a miserable, miserable place if everyone were a 4.0 with honors Ivy League medical doctor. The world needs me, and the world needs you. But the world needs the best version of you.

So, meditate on what the best version of yourself looks like, and act in ways in accordance with that version of you. I may want ice cream and potato chips every night, but is that what the best version of myself desires?

If you need an easy-to-read starting point, I recommend *Benjamin Franklin's Book of Virtues*, a brief overview of how to be a better version of yourself.

"It is amazing what you can accomplish if you do not care who gets the credit." President Harry Truman knew that achievements done for public approval are much less substantial than those done simply for the achievement itself.

The act of needing credit puts limitations on one's creativity and personal strengths. So the next time you do one thing, remember that everything you've ever done is a bunch of one things stacked together.

Act as the best version of yourself, like the most important thing in your world is the present action—not caring if you are ever rewarded or appreciated for the action. I guarantee this will lead to a step toward success.

Go get it, but get it because it brings you genuine joy, not because you want an outcome. Acting out of passion, no matter the outcome, is power.

Being detached from outcomes is an easy way to improve your life today. Work hard because you love the work, not because you want a promotion. Treat your spouse with love and kindness because that's who you are, not because you want something in return. Share wisdom and care because it's the right thing to do, not because you want credit or influence.

YOU ARE SPECIAL

I know, it's cheesy and overused. But the world needs you to be special—to be you, warts and all.

There's no other human in the world with your sphere of influence, your characteristics, and your specific opportunities to use both. This is not a fluffy motivational speech; this is a concrete fact.

The world doesn't need another person fearful of becoming what they know they should become. We have enough limited people already; we don't need more.

So once you understand who you are, the characteristics and strengths you have, what you deeply value, and all the aspects of life you can influence, then comes the time for action.

One caveat: it is counterproductive to act before becoming self-aware and emotionally intelligent because action will primarily be pleasure-seeking.

For example, binging Netflix, eating junk food, having promiscuous sex, drugs and alcohol, deceitful behavior for selfish gain, and a lot of other things are pleasurable. But pleasure doesn't equal benefit.

"Remember, nothing external to you has any power over you. Do not allow the mind to be a slave to the senses or to surrender to pleasure." (Aurelius, Marcus. *Meditations*, trans. Gregory Hays, Modern Library, 2002, p. 64.)

The world needs you to create more than you consume. Consuming media, screen time, and information is fine if it is not done in excess. Consuming anything for educational purposes is more beneficial than consuming for entertainment, while creating is the most beneficial.

The best version of you is a creator. Creating can look like many things.

You can write personally or publicly, create videos or lessons about things you are good at, create memories for yourself or those close to you, build literally anything, design an app, create a website, start a business, volunteer, get involved in a group that shares the same passion you do—so many more things.

The world doesn't need any more leeches sitting on the couch waiting for their next hit of happiness. The world needs you to create something from your heart.

Pleasure doesn't equal benefit; benefit equals benefit. What does it look like to act beneficially?

There is great power and freedom in knowing what you want and putting in the work to get it. If you've made it this far, then your character and moral compass are the driving forces in your mind.

So, you can trust your gut instincts and your desires, and you better know that the world needs you to get those desires.

I do not have to worry about any of you wanting wealth and acting on this desire by robbing a bank. A person with self-awareness who knows who they are can trust the desires they have and feel fully confident to act on them.

During grade school exams, we were all told to go with our gut and pick the first answer we thought was right. This does have truth and is double effective when the impulse to choose is met with confident wisdom and understanding of the principles discussed in this book.

My grandfather's wise words still ring true. When you know who you are and what you stand for, when you understand how you are influential, and when you have the goal to be the best version of yourself, then go for what you want without fear or second thoughts.

And going after what I want, because I know who I am, is what I wish I knew before I screwed my life up.

CHAPTER 6

THERE ARE NO MISTAKES

Think back to a time when you made a big mistake. Not just a small one like using bleach with colors in the wash (guilty), but a mess-up with some real repercussions. Now think of that mistake through the lens described by Ryan Holiday in his wonderful book *The Obstacle Is the Way*.

Take this mistake and pretend it's not important—like it doesn't matter. Act as if it's happening to someone else, and think of all the ways that you could solve the problem. You'll come to find thinking that the mistake was not a big deal robs the mistake of its power. It puts the power back in your hands and gives your mind the freedom to use the mistake to accomplish solutions.

This reframing perception is important. All bad things that happen to you in life arc only bad if you label them as

47

such. Every circumstance, even one with the magnitude of death or bodily injury, can be used for growth.

Everything in existence is in the past, present, or the future. The first is a set of beliefs, the second is the only actual thing we can tangibly attain, and the third is an infinite number of possibilities. Perception dictates reality.

As we've already seen, how we perceive an event determines what the event actually was. An event could be seen as a tragedy that leads to pain and suffering or could lead to growth and prosperity. The event is the same in both cases; the only difference is the perspective and perception of the past event.

Taking this a step further, every mistake you and I have ever made is only a mistake if we label them as such. Each mistake has been a brick in the road that led you to exactly where you are today. If that mistake didn't happen, then you would not be who you are today.

Define "Mistake"

The word mistake itself comes with negative connotations. Much in the same way that in the medical field, the word *shot* comes with negative connotations—such as pain and suffering—but in actuality, it can be lifesaving.

A person could either think they are being stabbed harmfully by a sharp object or that their life is being mercifully saved. The difference is because of a person's understanding and perception of the same event.

So, let's reframe that mindset. Every past mistake has already happened; there is no changing that. The DeLorean time machine isn't a possibility, so time travel to the past is not an option.

Einstein's relativity showed that we can travel to the future, but not by magic or wormholes—by altering physical perception and conditions compared to the world around us. Most of us time travel to the future each night by about 8 hours. Not by magic but by perception.

So, if every past mistake has happened and there is no way to alter this, each mistake is an integral part of who you are and how you think today. Take it from author and poet Ralph Waldo Emerson: "All life is an experiment. The more experiments you make, the better." (*Essays: First Series*, James Munroe & Co., 1841, p. 12.)

The idea that every mistake is simply a lesson and an opportunity to grow is not a new one. What's revelatory to me—and hopefully to you—is this new understanding that the past can't be changed, and a past in which you did not make this mistake is not a reality.

A present in which you did not make this mistake is also not a reality and will never be. Fantasizing about a past where a mistake didn't happen and a present or future that could be different is a counterproductive waste of energy.

It will prevent you from breaking free of the metaphorical chains holding your best self captive. *Had I only made that shot, had I only said that to the person in the meeting, had I only treated my spouse better, had I only*

49

worked harder, had I only spent more time with my kids, if only I would have gone to that thing, if only, if only.

Fantasizing about different outcomes may be momentarily pleasurable, but they are only that—a fantasy. Instead of dwelling on what could have been, learn and make something that could be.

The great Roman emperor and Stoic philosopher Marcus Aurelius knew this better than most. "If you are pained by any external thing, it is not this thing that disturbs you, but your own judgment about it. And it is in your power to wipe out this judgment now." (*Meditations*, trans. Gregory Hays, Modern Library, 2002, p. 55.)

So, wipe out the judgment of anything as a mistake and see them as "miss takes." I have good news: if you have breath in your lungs, you get another take.

What Is Real?

Try to think of something that doesn't have an end. All songs have an end—some mercifully. Anything created by humans has an end. All elements and substances will end, even the ones that can last billions of years. The universe and time itself will more than likely end.

So, if everything ends and the only variable deciding factor is time, and time is subjective based on perception, then is everything subjective and based on perception?

At the very least, all experiences end, as well as all success stories and all failures. With this foundation, perhaps all experiences are just practice for the next experience.

This isn't pointing toward nihilism but is a proponent of the belief that each mistake is only practice for the next encounter. Your next mistake will also be practice for the future.

"Nothing gold can stay." (Frost, Robert. "Nothing Gold Can Stay." *The Poetry of Robert Frost*, ed. Edward Connery Lathem, Henry Holt and Company, 1979, p. 222.) All things, whether good or bad, will inevitably end.

An example to try and illustrate this point: a man in 1900 entered a pub in England and said hello to the barkeep. A couple sitting at the bar saw this and nodded with approval. It was clear to them that this was a reality and actually happened.

No one would ever question that. But what about after these four witnesses to the event pass away and no one has any memory of that happening? Did it still actually happen? Well, of course.

But if no one living has any perception it actually happened, then is there any meaning or purpose for it happening? If a tree falls in the forest and no one hears it or ever sees that tree, then did it make a sound? Yes. But does that sound pertain to humanity at all? You be the judge.

And if something pertains to humanity, is the question of whether it actually happened or not one that will ever be raised?

The point here is what actually matters? We will get to that in a later chapter, but for now, let's use an example most people would say is significant: Harry Truman's decision to drop atomic bombs on Hiroshima and Nagasaki.

In his mind, this decision was not a mistake, but I can imagine in the minds of many on the island of Japan, it was a big mistake. Again, the definition of a mistake is defined by the person perceiving it.

Now, let's take the English pub logic and apply it to this much bigger decision. What happens when everyone with any recollection of World War II passes away? What happens when humanity goes extinct from the earth?

Will Harry Truman's decision be real or matter then? That time is inevitably coming, and we have seen that time is based on subjective perception. So, one could conceivably subjectively perceive that Truman's decision is unimportant at all right now.

And if that large of a decision will ultimately not matter, then all the mistakes you've ever made will ultimately not matter. So don't be afraid to make another one. Go for it.

A word about subjective individual truth versus absolute truth. While perception dictates how someone sees a situation, any situation or choice that involves another living being is ultimately judged by a moral criterion.

I could perceive that my decision to throw a rock through my neighbor's window will ultimately not matter in 200 years, but I still have a moral obligation to respect and honor one's right to life, liberty, and the pursuit of happiness—as stated by Thomas Jefferson in the United States Declaration of Independence.

I will leave the complexities of morality to the likes of Aristotle, Kant, Mill, and many others. But even understanding that a mistake is not a mistake, one has a moral duty to uphold certain standards.

As renowned 18th-century philosopher Immanuel Kant states in his Principle of Humanity of the categorical imperative: "Act in such a way that you treat humanity, whether in your own person or in the person of any other, never merely as a means to an end, but always at the same time as an end." (*Groundwork of the Metaphysics of Morals*, trans. Mary Gregor, Cambridge University Press, 1998, p. 38.)

This is important to note, but ultimately, becoming the best version of yourself will benefit society as a whole. As well as those near you, treating humanity as an end and not merely a way will come naturally to you.

There is freedom in seeing a mistake as not a mistake. This freedom allows confidence and assurance in future choices, knowing that even the wrong choice isn't the wrong choice. It simply puts you on the path that you are meant to be on.

There's only one reality: a reality where $2 + 2 = 4$, and a reality where you have made mistakes, and those mistakes have led you to where you are today. A reality where all your future mistakes will put you on the road you will be on.

You can choose one future path, but you can't change it. There are no alternate roads. There are no realities where you didn't make those mistakes.

Let the past mistakes go. Let the future possible mistakes go. Live in the present. And ironically, releasing the possibility of making a mistake will lead to a life filled with peace and joy.

Lying on your deathbed will let you look back at all the "failures" and "successes" in your life as puzzle pieces that played a role in your life story. All the pieces are needed, and none can be replaced. There is power and beauty in every choice you make.

And there is peace in accepting each choice as good. And that peace is what I wish I felt before I screwed my life up.

CHAPTER 7

WHAT REALLY MATTERS

I like going to concerts. I enjoy feeling like part of a group that is excited and unified about the same thing. I like the pageantry of the lights and the beautiful melody of the sounds. But would I go to a concert if I was the only one in attendance?

At first, you may think that would be an amazing, private show for one. But I'm talking about a typical concert that doesn't give special treatment. The band doesn't recognize you; staff members do not give special treatment besides front-row seating; you walk in and walk out of the arena like any common fan. This scenario doesn't sound too pleasant, does it? So, disregarding the hypothetical special VIP celebrity treatment, having other people around is a big draw for the desire to go to a concert.

Humans are designed with a need for community. In addition, we get a big rush of positive endorphins when that community aligns with our viewpoints. Social psychologist Jonathan Haidt describes this as tribalism:

> "Human beings are 90 percent chimp and 10 percent bee. We have a hive switch—a group-related adaptation that can turn us into team players, ready to dissolve our personal identity in service of the larger group. This is the psychology behind tribalism and the deep-seated need to belong to a group."
>
> *(Haidt, Jonathan. The Righteous Mind: Why Good People Are Divided by Politics and Religion. Pantheon Books, 2012, p. 220.)*

This is why solitary confinement for a prolonged period is one of the cruelest nonviolent forms of punishment a human can endure. The dream of living alone on an island and getting mail delivered once a month by ferry may sound like a nice fantasy, but it would really lead to a loss of purpose and feelings of sadness. We feel like we need to belong.

I also like to feel desired. The feeling of being loved by another human being is unparalleled. Human nature craves intimacy. It's why people get married; it's why people kiss, it's why we feel connected to one another when that connection doesn't make sense, it's why serotonin is released after physical contact with another human being.

Our hero, Viktor Frankl, describes love as the only way to grasp another human being in the innermost core of his personality. No one can become fully aware of the very essence of another human being unless he loves him (Frankl, p. 116).

German psychoanalyst Erich Fromm calls love the only sane and satisfactory answer to the problem of human existence. Without love, humanity could not exist for a day. *(Fromm, Erich. The Art of Loving. Harper Perennial Modern Classics, 1956, p. 25.)*

So, can we reasonably conclude that two things that actually matter are 1) how we are loved and how we love others and 2) the community of people we are involved in? I believe so.

But as we said before, all things must end, even love and connection. And it is a credible subjective perspective to believe that things that end do not truly matter. But what if these things did not end?

TRUTH

With an understanding of the previous chapter—that all failures will ultimately end and, at some point, have no real meaning or value—one can deduce that the only entity with true meaning would last forever.

Is there a way to concretely prove without a shadow of a doubt that anything eternal exists? Probably not. But in scientific theory, proving something is often less important than providing a concept that is more plausible than not.

For example, to say that all matter is made up of protons, neutrons, and electrons is a theory that's more plausible than not. Hypothetically, in 200 years, scientists could discover that each atom is made up of much smaller particles that render protons, neutrons, and electrons obsolete.

One of the foundational questions of existence is what is truth? Not what do I believe, or what do I feel is true, or what do I think is true, but what is actual truth. Some truths are simple; I, Kent Garrett, am writing this book right now.

Some truths are complex: is the universe expanding, and if so, what is outside of the borders of the edge of the universe? Some truths hold the key to everything: where did life come from, what is the purpose of human life, do we have a soul and is it eternal, and how do we receive eternal life? These questions deserve extensive study.

Perhaps these questions are the most important questions to give effort to answering, even more important than questions such as what will I eat, where will I sleep, how can I make money? Because eating, sleeping, and making money will all end.

This isn't religious evangelism; this is a call to find truth beyond a reasonable doubt. This is me saying that one of the most important issues (if not the most important) in all of existence is to find what, if anything, is eternal.

And to find this essential truth you must understand why you believe what you believe. If someone is raised to believe a certain doctrine, then they will more than likely choose to believe that principle as true over others. But just because your parents believed something was true doesn't mean it is.

Also, the culture in which one lives influences what they believe as true, too, partially due to the tribal mentality stated above. But this also doesn't make it true. Personal desires and biases don't influence absolute truth.

I could want the edge of the universe to be filled with diamonds and the hottest flames possible, but that does not make it true. It may be comfortable for me to believe that none of our actions matter, and when we pass away, we turn into nothingness for the rest of time. But to find truth, I need to examine my motives for a belief.

Maybe I don't want responsibility or consequences for my thoughts and actions. The bottom line is knowledge of why you believe what you believe is important. And the best reason to believe is because it is true.

The wise words of Plato:

"This is the distinction between the wise and the ignorant: the wise know what is truth, while the ignorant only believe or imagine it."

(Plato. The Republic. Translated by Benjamin Jowett, Oxford University Press, 1888, Book V, p. 199.)

So do some textual criticism—that is, seeing what ancient texts are valid and what are most likely not. Devote a good amount of time to finding what is most likely true.

And don't get discouraged when there is not 100% absolute certainty. Because there never will be complete certainty.

Faith in anything requires a little belief in the uncertain. Take away your cultural and family biases, and find what is true for yourself. Because only things that are eternal actually matter.

Mansions end, money ends, human bodies end, social media ends, food ends, sports end, presidents end, wars end, almost everything ends.

But do love, connection, salvation, faith, influence, how you impact another, and the essence of our souls last forever? That's a question that you must find an answer to, not because anyone told you to, but because you found it to be true.

And truth is what I wish I knew before I screwed my life up.

CHAPTER 8

UNITY

Divisiveness and confrontation are everywhere. Why? Because they sell. Humans are innately drawn to conflict. If we see two people in a screaming match on the street, we automatically want to observe and know what's going on, though at a safe distance because of the fear for self-preservation discussed before.

Picture yourself walking by a magazine stand. You see two magazine covers. One has the headline reading "Two State Senators Have a Pleasant Conversation and Come to an Agreement." The other states, "Betrayal, an Affair, and a Plot for Murder. America's So-called Sweetheart Couple is Hiding a Big Secret." Which one are you more likely to instinctively grab?

Why is it that when something is posted on social media the top comments are usually ones disagreeing with what is posted? Why do we tune in to political debates but don't care for more than 5 seconds when a peace treaty is signed?

Tribal mentality runs deep. We feel the need to stand up and fight against ideas that differ from our point of view, but we usually give less importance to things that agree with our ideology. That's why there are a lot more protest marches than marches of gratitude.

People will band together and fight for an injustice they believe is occurring, but they are much less likely to unify and fight when everything is going the way they want it to. There wouldn't be much interest in a presidential election if all candidates had the same policies and opinions. But why do humans feel such passion towards things that are different but often display apathy in unity?

An unconstrained heart, the heart being all that makes a person a person, craves power, control, and authority. One of the most influential modern thinkers, German philosopher Friedrich Nietzsche, relates human desire to a need for power.

"What is good? All that heightens the feeling of power, the will to power, and power itself in man. What is bad? All that proceeds from weakness. What is happiness? The feeling that power increases — that resistance is overcome." (Nietzsche, Friedrich. *The Antichrist*. Translated by H.L. Mencken, Alfred A. Knopf, 1924, p. 127.)

The heart wants what it wants, and wisdom is realizing we must not trust our heart before we learn to control it.

POWER

Power can be physical, social, economic, or psychological. Power is the ability or capacity to influence, control, or direct the behavior of others, the course of events, or specific outcomes. We feel good when we have power. But even Spider-man knows that with great power comes great responsibility.

The Stanford Prison Experiment is one of the most famous psychological studies of recent history. It was conducted in August 1971 by Dr. Philip Zimbardo at Stanford University. In this experiment, participants were randomly assigned the roles of either jailhouse prisoner or guard. All the partakers knew that they were playing fictional roles.

The study was originally going to last two weeks but was terminated after six days because of the abuse of power by those assigned the role of prison guard. The guards quickly adopted authoritarian roles, exhibiting cruel and dehumanizing behavior towards the prisoners, who became passive, depressed, and stressed.

The study revealed how situational dynamics and assigned roles could lead to significant changes in behavior. (Zimbardo, Philip G. "Pathology of Imprisonment." *Society*, vol. 9, no. 6, 1972, pp. 4-8.)

This experiment highlights a key, often overlooked, factor of the human condition. While this study showed that social roles and titles can invoke an abuse of power, it goes even deeper. Humans have a proclivity for using many types of influence as domineering.

For example, someone with a large social media following may look down upon someone with a small following. A person whose job requires them to work strenuous hours can feel superior to someone with a more relaxed work schedule. A person who has never struggled with drug abuse may not empathize and could even feel contempt when dealing with someone in recovery.

This condition of measuring ourselves constantly against others is innate, but it does not have to be demeaning or vindictive.

As we covered earlier, fear is a motivator whether we like it or not. Fear can either be limiting or a tool we can use; the gift of fear can be used for the betterment of ourselves and those around us.

Fear-mongering is a useful tactic of influence and manipulation because humans will always have the basic fear of not having enough resources for survival. It's a simple instinct, expressed in the simplest of terms; for example, if Johnny across the street has a gallon of water, then that's one gallon of water I will never have.

If a man finds a wife, that's one fewer fish in the sea for me. It's why when we believe that there will be a shortage of something, the simplest of humans will run to the store or gas station and hoard that resource.

(This also ties into the principle we covered in an earlier chapter, finding truth, finding actual truth you know to be true, not because someone told you it was true.) We fear that if someone else has something, then that's something we do not have.

We fear that if a political party that doesn't share our viewpoints gets put in office, then we will lose something we hold dearly. While this last fear may be true in some extreme cases in the world, in most of the democratic world, your life will be the same no matter who's in office.

So why can't we unify? The animal world kills each other for food to survive. Humans are more civilized, barely, so we create conflict out of prideful fear. We are taught to fight for what's ours and protect what we have. But this mentality only furthers selfishness, anger, disdain, and a feeling of lack.

Instead, let us meditate on and live out the word of Anne Frank; visionary, inspiration, and holocaust survivor: "No one has ever become poor by giving."
(Frank, Anne. *The Diary of a Young Girl*. Translated by B.M. Mooyaart, Doubleday, 1952, p. 238.)

You will not lose what you need by giving it away. You will not become less of a person by understanding another party's viewpoint. You will not lose your influence by uplifting someone, even if just in your mind, who is of less status or influence than you are.

You will not become weak by holding your tongue. You will, however, show light in the darkness the next time an argumentative word is replaced with compassion. The universe, karma, good vibrations, Yahweh, or whatever you believe usually finds a way to take care of the humble, the meek, the givers of the world.

And let me be clear that, fortunately, the practical applications of these principles of unity will mainly come in the metaphysical and mental form. Sometimes, your neighbor will need a gallon of water, but more often, this neighbor will need you to give them the benefit of the doubt.

They need you to look at them as valuable, having worth and deserving of care and respect. They need you not to see them as a threat but to see them as someone longing for connection and inclusion.

This neighbor needs you to see the next divisive article or news headline and think to yourself, is this really something that directly affects me today? This neighbor may have differing political viewpoints and opposing opinions on certain topics, but our greatest threat and our greatest ally is each other.

Who is this neighbor, you might ask? It's me. I need you to be all these things. And so does everyone else you will ever encounter.

So next time you see or hear something you don't agree with, pause, take a deep breath, and look at that person as a scared little child clinging to the hope that if he acts out, then his needs will be met, and he won't have to worry about surviving.

We all could benefit by giving people we don't agree with a little more empathy and a little less challenge.

CHAPTER 9

NOTHING TO LOSE

Some of this chapter will be versions of themes discussed in earlier chapters with an added layer of depth and practical application. Buckle up.

"Once you have lost the fear of death, you are free." (Malcolm X. *The Autobiography of Malcolm X*. As told to Alex Haley, Ballantine Books, 1992, p. 376)

In the 1500s, Spanish conquistador Hernán Cortés led an expedition to the Aztec Empire, which is present-day Mexico. He landed on an unconquered coastline to seize the region. After arriving, Cortés made a determined and striking move to ensure his men were committed to the mission: he ordered the burning of his own ships. He knew that his fleet was outnumbered, and the mission was most likely going to be difficult, maybe even impossible. By removing the means of escape, the soldiers had a new powerful motivation to either move forward or die.

(Prescott, William H. *History of the Conquest of Mexico.* Edited by John Foster Kirk, J.B. Lippincott & Co., 1873.)

There were no other possible options. In the fantastic movie by Christopher Nolan, *The Dark Knight Rises* (although not as good as *The Dark Knight*), Christian Bale's Batman is imprisoned in an underground prison called "The Pit." The only chance of escape is to scale a tall, well-like wall and make a near-impossible jump to freedom with only a rope as a safety harness from assured death. After many failed attempts, one of the oldest prisoners tells Bruce Wayne the secret to escape: jump without the rope.

The psychology of having no safety net activates a powerful primal motivation. Much like an adrenaline-raged mother lifting a heavy car off her child, this motivation releases abilities far beyond what the person thought they were capable of. Athletes have the win-or-go-home mentality, meaning winning is the only option. The mother sees no other option when her child's life is in danger. Cortés's men knew they had only one option to survive. When there is only one path between success and failure, the way forward becomes clear.

This is wonderful as a psychological principle, but what does it look like for your practical application in everyday life? It may not be prudent to invest all of your resources into an entrepreneurial passion, but that might be exactly the right decision. Henry Ford left a stable job to pursue his dream, and he was met with many failures and was on the brink of complete loss before finding success.

(Ford, Henry. *My Life and Work*. Garden City Publishing, 1922.)

But for every Ford story, there are many more stories of failure. Building off the principle that mistakes aren't mistakes, are failures really failures? For every person who took a leap of faith and failed, I don't believe that they actually failed. Even in the extreme case that their "failure" resulted in temporary (or permanent) homelessness and poverty, they still didn't fail.

The homeless man no one knows and Warren Buffett both end up six feet in the ground with a long path of experiences behind them, one not better than the other. Think of every success and failure as a puzzle piece that makes up part of the mosaic of life. Each one is just as necessary and beautiful as the other.

COMFORT

Comfort breeds weakness. Growth happens outside your comfort zone. This is a radical concept but not a complex one. It is easy to work a stable job, do things that are familiar and secure, make sure your actions please most people, and never rock the boat. But is this the best version of yourself? This doesn't mean always stir up controversy and cause problems.

Ford made the radical decision to start a motor company but also didn't blow it up and start from ground zero when it was successful or when a co-worker pissed him off. So, the prescription for you is different depending on where you are in life. It's not a one-size-fits-all. But it is a feeling deep in the pit of your heart that you know you need to do. I can't tell you how and when to get out of your comfort zone. But you can; you already know what this looks like.

It's there deep in your heart; go for it.

So what's holding you back? What's keeping you from doing the thing or becoming the person you know deep in your soul you need to be? It's probably the perspective of having something to lose. It's the perspective of having a lifeline or a safety net. Playing not to lose the game differs greatly from playing to win.

A person living not to lose something will more than likely lose it. And the person playing to win will more than likely win. Think of everything you have as a borrowed gift, a temporary pleasure you must return at some point. Even wealth left to your future generations, while being a good thing, will eventually be given back. You literally have nothing to lose because nothing is yours anyway. Think of doing the next hard thing as practice.

» Asking for a raise or quitting your job, practice for your next job.
» Learning an instrument or putting your singing voice online, practice to become bold and unashamed.
» Putting down electronics and spending a week in nature, practice to be more grounded and present.

» Confronting someone who is repeatedly disrespectful to you, practice confrontation and understanding.

» Dealing with a breakup or losing someone or something dear to you, practice to gain fortitude and cope with grief.

» Taking a position or hobby for less pay, practice going after your passion above chasing the dollar.

When you think of all events and experiences simply as practice to get better for the next one, the limits you put on yourself will slowly start to disappear. Boldness will become a natural feeling. Fear of loss will start to fade away slowly because there is usually little, if anything, to lose.

CHAPTER 10

YOU ARE WHAT YOU ARE

Everything you will ever do is an attempt to answer a question, address a need, or find a solution to a problem. This includes individual and corporate actions. A state or local government's actions attempt to find a solution to a problem, but with questionable motives at times.

Getting a job solves a money and purpose need. Watching TV answers the need for relaxation and detachment. Rolling over in bed, solving positional un-comfortability. Talking to another person addresses the need for human interaction or to gain a resource. The list goes on and on.

Each individual has slightly different answers to the same questions in different circumstances. Part of the human experience is that we are all asked the same questions. Who we are, what we need, how we find peace, what gives us meaning, and how we interact with the world are questions we all must answer. The key is finding your best answer to each question and not believing your answer is wrong because it differs from someone else's.

The great white shark is an apex predator. Revered for its ability to end the life of anything it desires. It moves with ferocity; just the sight of it sends shivers down the spine. But ask the shark to go up one flight of stairs in an apartment building, and the shark will not seem so intimidating. You may be a shark, but you haven't found your ocean. Or even worse, you've been trying to climb stairs because that's what you see other people doing.

If you've made it this far in this book, then you probably have a pretty good understanding of who you are, what your strengths are, your goals, and, most important, what makes you who you are.

Using this wisdom, the next steps are to appreciate and applaud your strengths while also giving yourself grace and learning from your weaknesses. A shark doesn't care it can't climb stairs, but it would be prudent for you to understand your weaknesses and use them to your advantage.

When you notice a weakness, or you feel you did something wrong, do not shame yourself, but gently use self-talk to understand why this happened and what you can learn from it. For example, I usually have less social confidence and charisma in loud group settings with background musical noise. So, I intentionally avoid interactions like this for long periods and try to provide alternative social events that bring out my strengths deliberately.

I understand and use this weakness to my advantage instead of letting it make me feel like I'm not enough. I talk to myself as a loving friend would talk to another. I will never be the life of the party or Mr. Entertainment, but I can make someone feel very heard and understood in one-on-one conversation. I can naturally shift the focus from myself to the other person so well that Dale Carnegie himself would be proud. I appreciate my strength and seek to highlight it.

BOLD SECURITY

Building on this understanding of what makes you who you are and appreciating your strengths while learning from your weaknesses, the next step is to find bold security and confidence in who you are. This may be the most difficult thing mentioned in this entire book, but it is equally important.

I spent years comparing myself to other people and feeling inferior to them. I wanted to be more socially outgoing and fun. I looked at guys all around me who were loud and entertaining and always had something to say, and I wanted to be like them. I was a shark trying to climb stairs.

Feeling inadequate because you don't match up to someone is one of the easiest things the human brain can do. But it's also one of the most destructive. Why do we do this so instinctively? Comparison gives us an outlet to feel self-pity, to settle for mediocrity, and not motivate ourselves to move forward. It creates a pit of despair and inadequacy. This contrasts with healthy competition in which a person celebrates the victories of others and uses them as motivation to succeed without manipulating people as a means to an end.

> "When we compare ourselves to others, we often judge ourselves based on their strengths rather than our unique qualities. This can lead to feelings of inadequacy and low self-esteem, as we focus on what we lack rather than what we possess."
>
> —Brown, Brené. *The Gifts of Imperfection*, p. 92

Embrace who you are. The homeless man is no better or worse than the CEO because of a title or status. If you're quiet and empathetic, then be that; who cares if the loud person who doesn't really listen is getting all the attention? That's not you, and it shouldn't be.

If you have the gifts of charisma and outgoing boldness, embrace them and be thankful to all the people who listen to you and let you express your strengths. If you have social anxiety and don't value having an online presence, admire that about yourself and give back to the world through whatever strengths you have.

Whatever you are, be that. It doesn't matter what fake highlight reel you see online or what public persona you desire. Be you, not what you think someone else wants you to be.

Actor Jim Carey achieved fame, success and public exaltation. He found out that it wasn't enough. In a speech to a graduating Maharishi University class, he said,

"I think everybody should get rich and famous
and do everything they ever dreamed of so they
can see that it's not the answer."

It's not the answer to peace, purpose, or happiness. The answer lies within. It may sound cliché, but it is the damn truth.

The answer comes when you know who you are and why you are that way, and you accept and admire that about yourself. Really admire your strengths because no one else in the world has your strengths in your situations. You are the only person in existence who will ever affect the world exactly how you do. Don't deprive your world of that by trying to be like someone else.

A quick note on learning. From the moment we're born, we are constantly learning from another human being. This learning doesn't come with envy until much later in life. Learning is healthy; imitation can also be healthy. But comparison with disdain or jealousy is not.

So, learn from people. But learn so you can become a better version of yourself to make the world around you a little bit better place.

So, what is the culmination of all the in-depth psychological tricks and philosophical insights we have studied?

I agree with Ralph Waldo Emerson when he answered that question:

"To be yourself in a world that is constantly trying to make you something else is the greatest accomplishment."

—Ralph Waldo Emerson, *Self-Reliance*, 1841

Be yourself, your true self, especially when the world tries to take that away. Anything less deprives the world around you of the beauty only you can offer.

Ask yourself out loud right now:

Who is "insert your name"?

Write down your answers and start admiring that about yourself today.

CONCLUSION

There you have it, ten things to know so you don't screw your life up like I did. But even by screwing my life up, I didn't screw it up. I just put myself on the path that led me to where I am today and to where I will go tomorrow. And that is not a mistake. My life is not screwed up, it never was, and it never will be. The same goes for you.

So, let's recap what secrets were revealed.

We learned that fear is a powerful and necessary motivator. Fear, seen as a gift, can be used for growth and success. Once anxiety is understood, then it loses its crippling effect and becomes a tool able to be manipulated however needed. Failure is only a failure if you consider it that way. Every single failure or mistake viewed as a productive learning experience is no longer a failure or mistake.

The most destructive actions are inaction, followed by regret and guilt. Avoid inaction, and use the motivation to avert regret as a catalyst for bold action. Let self-assurance and wisdom guide where doing nothing is doing something.

Peace follows presence. Chasing the greener grass will lead to a never-ending rat race of discontentment. Living in the present is the only way to be in reality. The past is a set of beliefs, and the future is theoretical endless possibilities that most likely will never happen.

Achievement-based identity is a lie that culture tells us that involves finding identity and self-worth through accomplishments. True self-worth is found in appreciation of the qualities that you already have that make you who you are.

Trying to find the perfect choice will paralyze the chooser and cause the best choices not to be chosen. The paradox of choice shows that one should strive for a sufficient choice and be content with whatever choice is made. Happiness is found when you deeply appreciate whatever choice is made and make an intentional effort to see the best in the decision.

Understanding the why behind your actions and desires is important to understanding who you are. Recognizing why you are who you are will bring a deep sense of purpose to one's life.

The two-day terminal diagnosis reveals one's true desires and those desires should be what you are working toward today. The story of the concentration camp prisoners highlights the importance of perspective on hope and meaning. Why they found meaning is an important question to ask. They chose to focus on how their actions affected and influenced others, what they could control, and how

S. Kent Garrett

temporary life is. This perception allowed for an increased sense of purpose.

Joy was very much a real thing during an inhumane, life-threatening camp life, and joy can be very much a real thing for you no matter what your circumstances.

Focusing on what you want but don't have leads to a feeling of inadequacy and defeat. Shifting the mental focus toward the things you have, even if just basic things, such as breath in the lungs or legs that work, allows for feelings of gratitude. This mentality helps to facilitate peace.

Like I was dissatisfied with my birthday party because I wanted a gift I didn't have, when we desire what we do not currently have, we are neglecting the present moment and robbing ourselves of happiness. Happiness is a choice, a choice not to put identity into chasing after things that will have no value in 50 years. Choosing to appreciate all life offers, both hardships and triumphs, is the secret to happiness.

Every decision ever made could have been thwarted by someone falling into the unknown of the what-ifs. The story of my grandfather's advice to get the knife I desired highlights the principle of action in the face of uncertainty.

Always try to discern between what you can directly control and what you should simply know. Self-awareness lets a person look inside themselves and know what virtues they hold dear. Self-assurance leads to bold determined action in upholding these virtues and values.

Self-appreciation comes from believing you are virtuous, that you are special, and no one in history will have the exact same gifts and sphere of influence you do. When a person has these three virtues of self-wisdom, their desires and actions will fall in alignment with what is beneficial for themselves and those in their sphere of influence.

To maximize growth, we must reframe our perception of what a mistake is. Many decisions could be viewed as a great success or a huge mistake, depending on perception. If we give ourselves grace and understand that even the worst of our past mistakes attempted to do the thing we thought best at the moment, then we can take power from the mistake and give it back to ourselves.

A mistake viewed as a learning experience becomes a learning experience. A mistake viewed as a failure becomes a failure. A wise person uses each past decision as constructive feedback for future possibilities. A person has only one path in life. The quicker you come to appreciate the path you're on and the mistakes that led you there, the more beautiful that path becomes.

"What really matters" and "What is truth" are two of the most important foundational questions that a human can ever ask. Of similar importance is how a person comes to find these answers and why they believe them to be true.

Like the principle of the movie *Inception*, a person who comes upon an idea by their own volition will be much stronger grounded than if they are told this idea is true by an outside source. Things that end will inevitably not matter in time. Eternal things, however, do not have an expiration. The task is to voyage on a journey to find things eternal.

Faith requires belief even when there is some doubt. All theories and beliefs have at least some level of doubt. The key is to find the truth beyond a reasonable doubt. Is the human soul and its interaction with other souls real and eternal? That's a truth that I have found the answer to, but it's one you must find on your own.

Modern culture manipulates conflict to motivate people in a biased direction. Left vs. right, Wade vs. Roe, our entire political system is based around one person losing and one winning. The desired outcomes of this division are usually power, control, influence, or money.

Unity, harmony, and love do not sell. That's why fear-mongering and mass media are predicated upon our innate desire for survival. It is easy to follow the herd mentality and think that if someone else is gaining a resource then that is a resource you will never have.

Luckily, in most of the modern world, this is not the case. There is plenty for everyone. And even if there isn't enough, it would be beneficial for you and society to learn how to create this resource.

The world does not need more anger towards each other; the world needs you to be kind to your neighbor who has something you don't have or believes something you don't believe. When all else fails, be kind. Try to understand another person's heart with kindness and humility.

Holding tightly with the fear of losing something will usually result in that thing being lost. But letting go of ownership of that thing and realizing that it is only, at the most, temporarily yours will paradoxically either let you own and appreciate that thing or will release you of the desire for it. Either way will result in freedom.

When you view all physical things as temporary, only then will you understand that there is no need to fear loss because ultimately, all things will be lost. You live, and you lose. And losing things is a beautiful necessary part of life.

So, instead of putting your identity into what you have or what you want, look at all events as practice for the next one. Even amateur athletes are less nervous in an isolated practice than they are in the real game. So, view everything you will do from this day forward as your practice to become a better version of yourself.

You are special; I am special. Because you are who you are, and I am who I am. We lose a little of our unique beauty when we try to conform to some image we see online or that we see getting praised.

There is pain and suffering from viewing yourself as incomplete, needing to change to be accepted and appreciated. There is peace and joy when you can appreciate who you are. When you are confident in what you have to offer while also having the humble wisdom to know that you will always have many things to learn and many ways to grow.

A shark is no match for a canary if the canary is on the second floor of an apartment building. You may be a shark; you just need to find your ocean. And when the world tries to tell you, you will never be good enough unless you learn how to climb stairs, block out the noise. Find your ocean.

There is a lot of psychological, philosophical, and cultural information in this book. But it doesn't mean a whole lot if you just read it to understand it. This book is designed to be put into practice.

Remember, when reading this book or any book, you should think about three things:

1. what does this mean,
2. how can I use it, and
3. when will I use it?

Go back at your leisure over the chapters and practice putting these principles into use in your life.

Contact me with any stories or questions about the material, with kindness and Kant's principle of humanity in mind, of course. I wish you the most favor in your journey to becoming the best version of yourself.

Do not minimize your importance or your influence. You matter. If you don't believe anything else, believe that your words and actions matter a lot to those around you but also yourself. People need you. And if you remember that, you will never screw your life up.

S. Kent Garrett, B.S. M.A., is a lifelong student of philosophy, psychology, theology, and self-improvement. After dropping out of DPT school, he battled and eventually overcame alcohol addiction. This addiction led to many failed relationships and destroyed friendships. After years of suffering and failures, he slowly learned the secrets to happiness and success shared in this book. He now works as a counselor for medical patients going through trauma in Nashville, Tennessee.

NOTES

NOTES

NOTES

NOTES

NOTES

NOTES

NOTES

NOTES

NOTES

NOTES

www.ingramcontent.com/pod-product-compliance
Lightning Source LLC
Chambersburg PA
CBHW071212120626
46546CB00006B/2531